BACKYARD WILDLIFE

Wolves

by Emily Green

BELLWETHER MEDIA • MINNEAPOLIS, MN

Note to Librarians, Teachers, and Parents:

Blastoff! Readers are carefully developed by literacy experts and combine standards-based content with developmentally appropriate text.

Level 1 provides the most support through repetition of high-frequency words, light text, predictable sentence patterns, and strong visual support.

Level 2 offers early readers a bit more challenge through varied simple sentences, increased text load, and less repetition of high-frequency words.

Level 3 advances early-fluent readers toward fluency through increased text and concept load, less reliance on visuals, longer sentences, and more literary language.

Level 4 builds reading stamina by providing more text per page, increased use of punctuation, greater variation in sentence patterns, and increasingly challenging vocabulary.

Level 5 encourages children to move from "learning to read" to "reading to learn" by providing even more text, varied writing styles, and less familiar topics.

Whichever book is right for your reader, Blastoff! Readers are the perfect books to build confidence and encourage a love of reading that will last a lifetime!

This edition first published in 2011 by Bellwether Media, Inc.

No part of this publication may be reproduced in whole or in part without written permission of the publisher. For information regarding permission, write to Bellwether Media, Inc., Attention: Permissions Department, 5357 Penn Avenue South, Minneapolis, MN 55419.

Library of Congress Cataloging-in-Publication Data
Green, Emily K., 1966-
  Wolves / by Emily Green.
    p. cm. – (Backyard wildlife)
Includes bibliographical references and index.
  Summary: "Developed by literacy experts for students in kindergarten through grade three, this book introduces wolves to young readers through leveled text and related photos"–Provided by publisher.
  ISBN 978-1-60014-563-6 (hardcover : alk. paper)
  1. Wolves–Juvenile literature. I. Title.
QL737.C22G7247 2011
599.773–dc22   2010034534

Printed in the United States of America, North Mankato, MN.
010111   1176

Contents

Wolves are
a kind of
wild dog.
Wolves are
mammals.

Wolves have thick fur and bushy tails. They stay warm in cold weather.

Wolves live in forests, grasslands, and **tundras**. They stay away from cities and people.

Most wolves live in groups called **packs**. A pack has between 4 and 10 wolves.

One male wolf and one female wolf lead a pack. They are called the **alpha pair**.

The pack has a **territory**. The wolves mark it with their **scent**.

A wolf pack hunts together. The wolves chase their **prey** until it gets tired.

Wolves hunt deer, moose, elk, and other animals. Old wolves work together to teach young wolves how to hunt.

Wolves **howl** to talk to each other when they hunt. Aaaooooooo!

Glossary

alpha pair—the male and female wolves that lead a pack

howl—a long, loud, sad sound

mammals—warm-blooded animals that have backbones and feed their young milk

packs—groups of animals that live and hunt together

prey—animals hunted by other animals for food

scent—the smell of an animal

territory—the area where an animal or group of animals lives and hunts

tundras—large, flat areas of frozen land without trees

wild dog—a member of the dog family that lives in nature

To Learn More

AT THE LIBRARY

Arnosky, Jim. *Wolves*. Washington, D.C.: National Geographic Society, 2001.

Berger, Melvin and Gilda. *Howl! A Book About Wolves*. New York, N.Y.: Scholastic, 2002.

George, Jean Craighead. *Look to the North: A Wolf Pup Diary*. New York, N.Y.: HarperCollins, 1997.

ON THE WEB

Learning more about wolves is as easy as 1, 2, 3.

1. Go to www.factsurfer.com.

2. Enter "wolves" into the search box.

3. Click the "Surf" button and you will see a list of related Web sites.

With factsurfer.com, finding more information is just a click away.

Index

The images in this book are reproduced through the courtesy of: Holly Kuchera, front cover; Jack Milchanowski/Photolibrary, p. 5; Klein-Hubert/KimballStock, pp. 7, 13, 17; Susann Parker/Photolibrary, p. 9; Lakov Kalinin, p. 9 (left, right); Juan Martinez, p. 9 (middle); Image100/Photolibrary, p. 11; Robert Franz/KimballStock, p. 15; J.L. Klein & M.L. Hubert/Photolibrary, p. 19; Gregory Johnston, p. 19 (left); Kirk Geisler, p. 19 (middle); Wesley Aston, p. 19 (right); Ron Kimball/KimballStock, p. 21.